tern on a tap

to Caroline

'Cast your bread upon
the waters and it will
come back
ham sandwiches'
(my father)

©2002 Simon Drew
World copyright reserved

ISBN 1 85149 425 1

British Library Cataloguing-in-Publication Data
A catalogue record for this book is available from the British Library

Published and printed in England by the Antique Collectors' Club Ltd., Woodbridge, Suffolk
on Consort Royal Satin from Donside Mill, Aberdeen, Scotland

her majesty with her lady in whiting

MARITIME PHRASES
a history

Few people realise how much we owe to ancient sailors for the richness of the english language. As an example, sailors used to cook in a stewpot known as a marmite (or 1 marmite) from which an anagram gives us the word maritime.

The phrase 'to put the cart before the horse' originally came from the naval expression: 'to put the carp before the oars'. (This is an example of a schoonerism).

fig. 1

If a sailor saw an unusual animal it wasn't long before he gave it a name:

.....A rare sighting would be an aggressive or vicious seal:

fig. 2

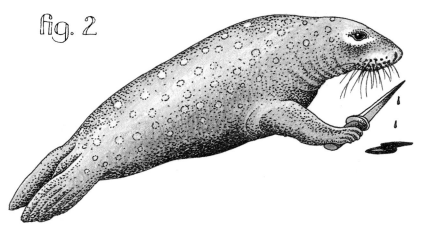

This was known as a Killer Seal and was thought to be the bringer of bad luck. Hence the expression we now use: Achilles heel.

When Sir Francis Drake was invited to a feast on board a dutch ship, he declined saying that he would not go to anything that might turn out to be a damp squid:

fig. 3

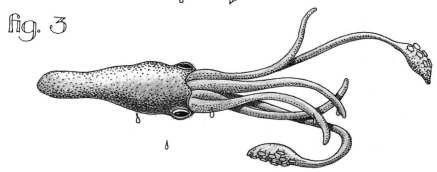

Some ancient mariners would never go to a party given by Sir Walter Raleigh. Although he gave many, he was known to be a miserly host who gave plenty to smoke but little wine. Hence the old sea shanty:

'Walter Walter everywhere
nor any drop to drink.'

When whaling began, ships would be sent to hunt down the biggest whales. However little is now known about Sir Percival Verdipax who tried to save these giant mammals by getting ahead of the whaling ships, netting the whales and then secretly taking them overland to a quiet bay to slip away. For this he invented a special means of transport still remembered today:

fig. 4
the whalebarrow

..... Magellan had to take out a particularly big loan from a bank for one of his voyages. The bank insisted that he registered how much he'd paid back on the rope with which he secured his ship to the harbour wall. This was called a moor-gauge; Magellan considered that he had borrowed so much he must have crossed the international debt-line.

Magellan sailed to far-off pacific islands where a form of mutton was preserved by salting it and pressing it into bottle-shaped guords. This gave rise to the expression: putting a sheep in a bottle.

fig.5

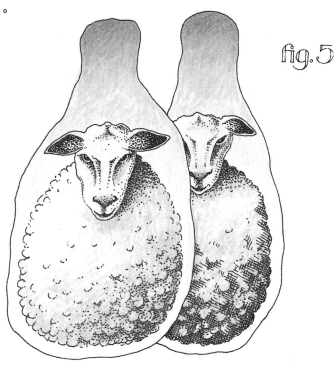

a tale of two settees

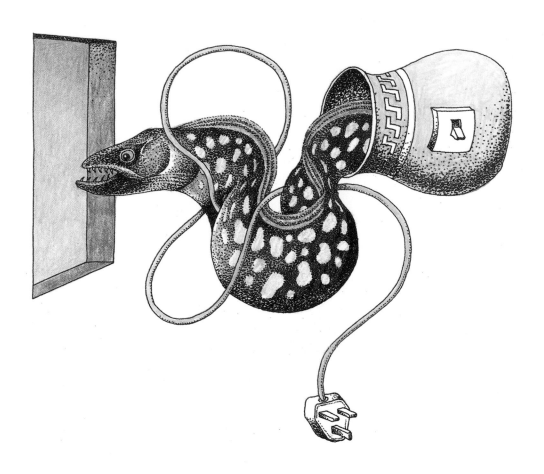

NO ONE BADLY INJURED

Many small fish were shocked
some of their jaws even locked:
though not very much was detected
an electric eel is suspected.

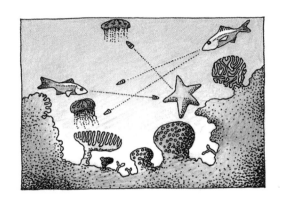

gunfight
at the OK coral reef

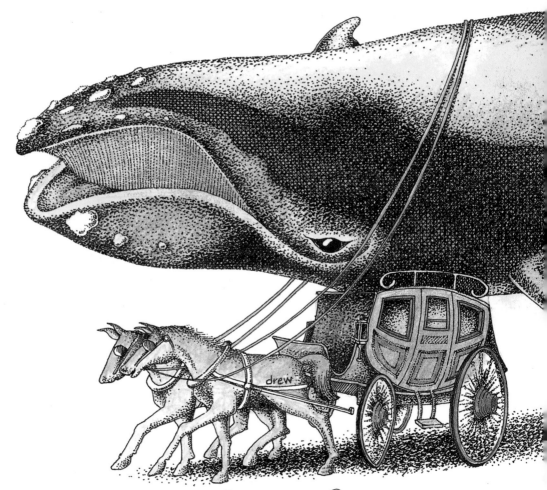

whales fargo

'I've got all the money I'll ever need,
if I die by 4 o'clock this afternoon.'
Henry Youngman

a circus poem:
A lion
B hind
C lions

waders of the lost ark

18

THE SEA BED

If a lobster can lie on a seabed
where are the sea pillows kept?
And if it is here in the daytime
where in the world has it slept?
If a willow can weep over water
how will we know if it's wept?
If a creeper can live on the willow
do we say, when it grows, it has crept?
If broom covers hillsides with yellow
how will they ever get swept?
If a frog can play leap-frog with no-one
how do we know when it's leapt?

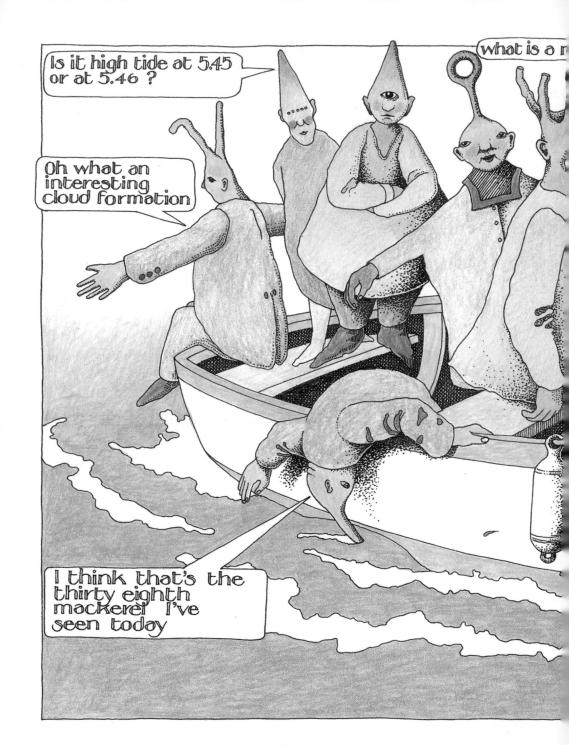

A HUNDRED AND ONE DULL MARTIANS

21

there are more old drunks
than old doctors

anon

the animals came in four-by-four

mallards, ladies and gentlemen

cod shave the queen

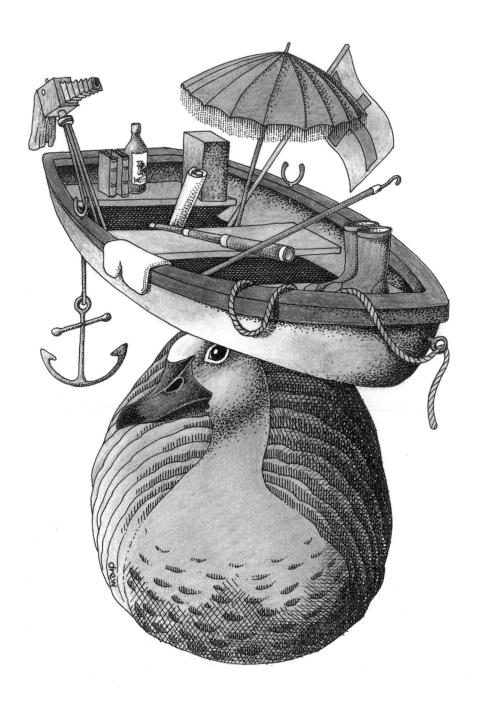

Needed on Voyage

Corkscrew, compass, anchor, sails,
thing to fire harpoon in whales,
boathook, biscuits, painters, rum,
thing to keep the sun off mum,
water, whisky, ice-cold beer,
thing to see when land is near,
rubber wellies, waterproofs,
thing to get the stones from hoofs,
starcharts, seacharts, satellite dish,
book to find the names of fish,
swimsuit, camera, dried food, flag:
put them all in one big bag.
Once you think you've got them all,
never leave the harbour wall.

PELICAN

PELICAN

30

OYSTER

How could an oyster
become any moister
if it lives at the bottom of the sea?
It could cry pearls of knowledge,
eat sloppy porridge
or drink very sweet milky tea.

But now you give it salt
or a bottle full of malt
or give it a chair beside the fire;
it would bring a look of grace
to that bivalve's little face
and soon the moister oyster
                    would get drier.

oyster dream moisturising cream

SPOT THE OCEANS AND SEAS

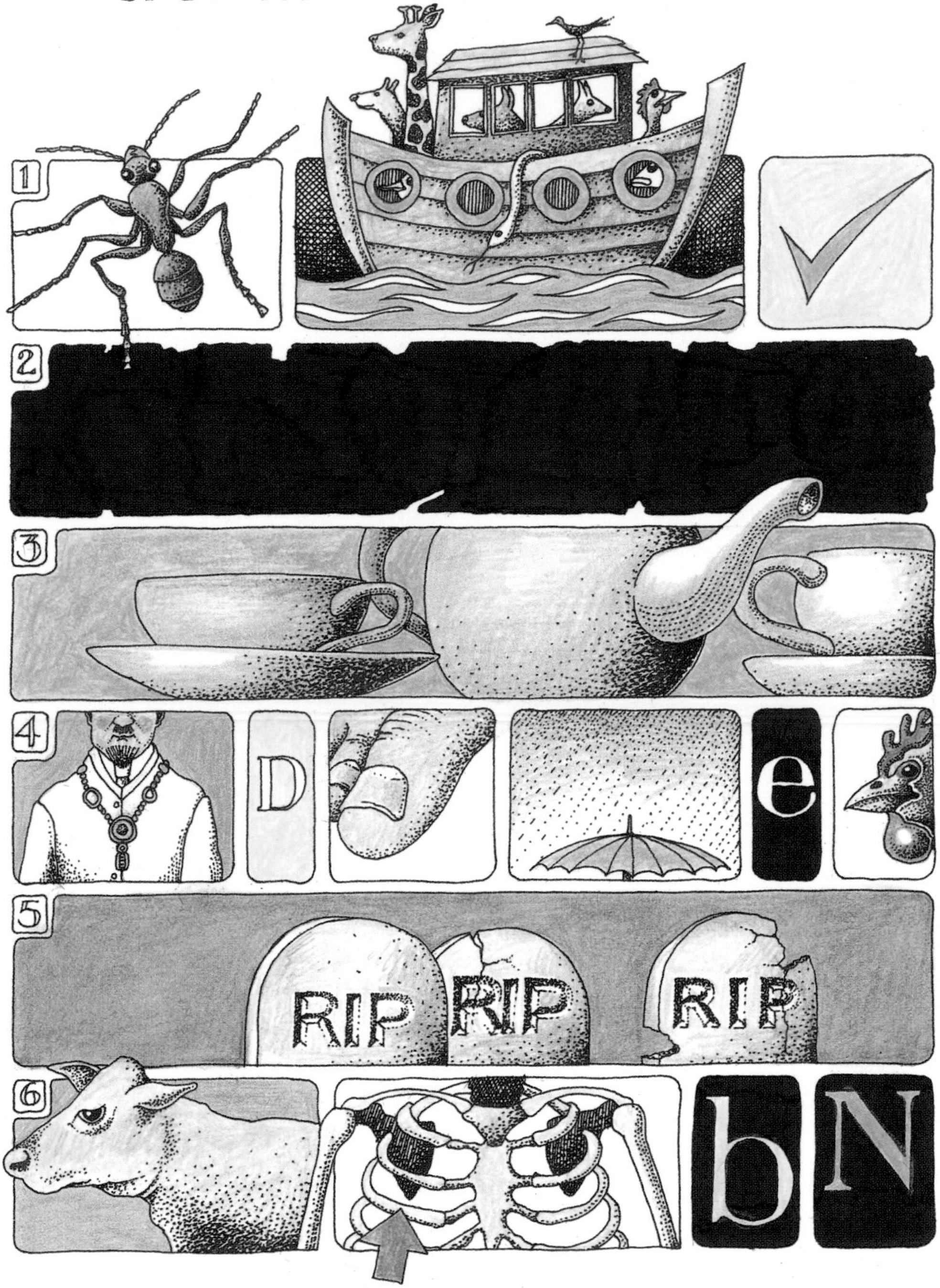

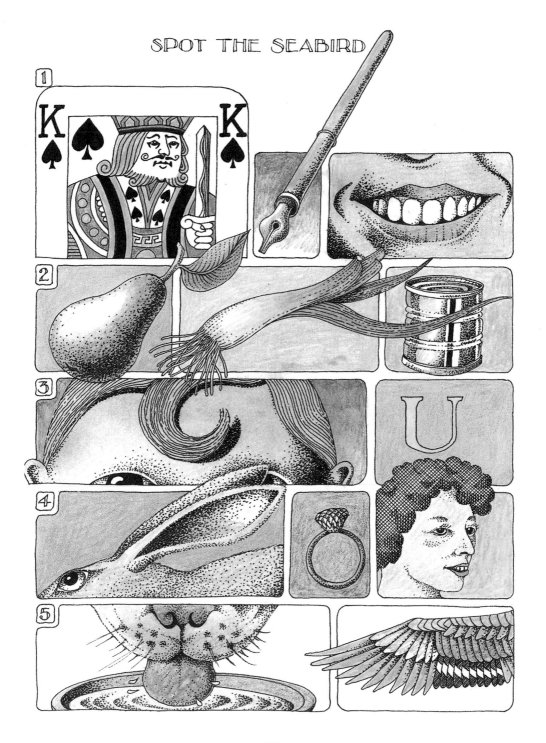

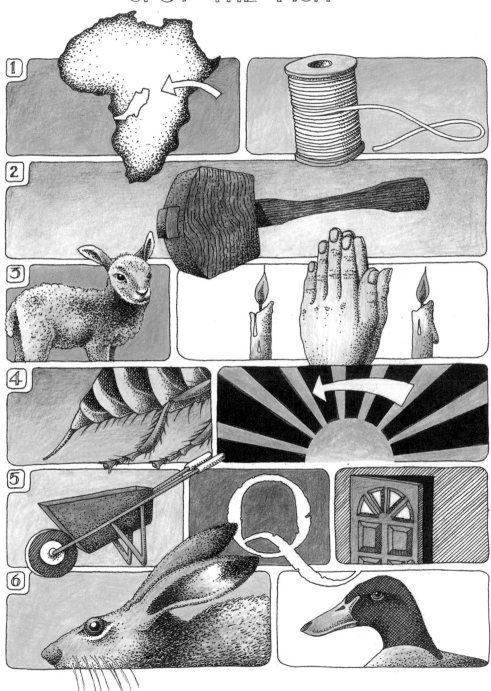

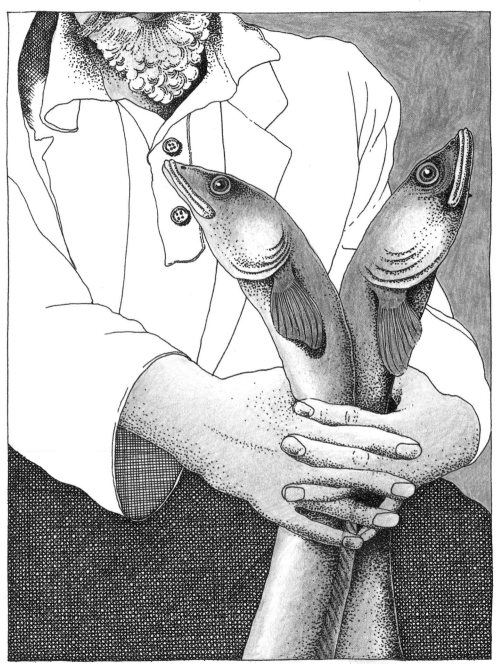

an old fisherman shows a clean pair of eels

gentlemen prefer ponds

matinée on the bounty

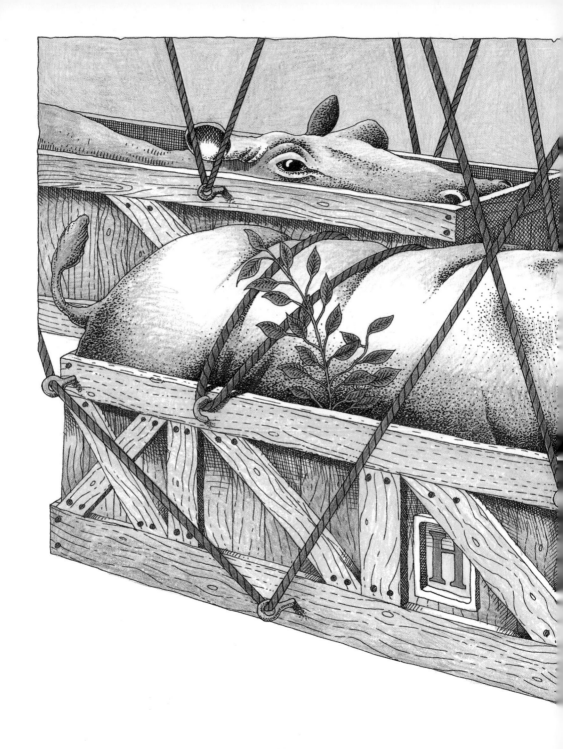

hippo crates

GOOD WISHES

.... to you on this great day,
May all your troubles fly away.
And so I send this thought to say:
Shame your birthday's not today.

tall sheep race

WHO MAKES THE NOISES AT SEA ?

When you're by the seaside
you'll hear a constant prattle,
sometimes just a rumbling
that sounds like far off cattle,
or maybe more a whispering
and then a short mock battle.
What you're really hearing
is turtle tittle-tattle.